Alfred JAZZ

PLAY ALONG SERIES

VOLUME 3

BRUBECK & MORE

9 JAZZ STANDARDS

FOR RHYTHM SECTION: PIANO, BASS, & DRUMSET

MP3 CD INSIDE

Alfred

BRUBECK & MORE
9 JAZZ STANDARDS
FOR RHYTHM SECTION: PIANO, BASS, & DRUMSET

CONTENTS

PIANO

BASS

DRUMSET

Performers: Tony Nalker—Piano; Paul Henry—Bass; Todd Harrison—Drums; Pete BarenBregge—Tenor Sax; Justin Kisor—Trumpet; Ben Patterson—Trombone

Sample solos composed by Rich Sigler.

Recorded at Bias Studio, Springfield, VA, Bob Dawson, engineer.

INTRODUCTION

The focus of this book is for piano, bass and drumset players to learn how to play in a rhythm section, comp behind horn players and work on their own improvisation. These nine jazz standards all have a melody and chord progression that is interesting to listen to, play and solo on. A point of interest is often generated from the movement of the chord progression to new temporary keys (not necessarily a key signature change), the use of colorful notes in the harmony, the harmonic chord progression and the way it moves to a bridge section, patterns, and so on. The written-out sample jazz solos are not necessarily a definitive solo but merely an example of how one can improvise on the chord progression

Playing jazz takes time: it involves learning your instrument, playing a variety of tempos, keys and rhythms, knowing about chords, scales and progressions. A book is a helpful guide to assist you but no book alone will make you an improviser. You will need to listen, practice, use your imagination, knowledge and ears to improvise!

Here are some general suggestions for creating an improvised solo:

1. **Listening.** This is absolutely essential to improvisation. You will gain skill from listening. We play music so people will listen to it. Listen and absorb, and you will be rewarded with knowledge.

2. **Hear it, Sing it, Play it!** Listen to each tune, the sample solo and the chord progression. Repeat this again and this time, sing the melody and the sample solo aloud. Repeat often. Listen for intervals and chord movement that appeals to you.

3. **Form.** Always know where you are in the form of the song. This is easy when playing the melody but can be a challenge when soloing. Listen for pivot chords—chords that will move your ear to a new section or a new key center. Pivot chords will help you keep your place in the form.

4. **Chords and scales.** At the minimum, learn the major, minor, Mixolydian and Dorian scales in all keys. The more you know about the notes in each chord and the related scale, the more knowledgeable and prepared you will be. Study and learn the notes in the chords, chord extensions and the scales that apply. However, one does not improvise by simply playing chord and scale notes. Chords and scales are tools to assist and guide you in creating your own improvisation. The 3rd and the 7th are the most important notes in a chord because they provide the harmonic identity. Space in this book does not permit further explanation of chords and scales. Chords and scale information can be learned from many other theory and improvisation books.

5. **Patterns.** Practice various patterns, especially ii-V patterns, and then apply them into your solos right away.

6. **Sound.** Always strive for a good sound on your instrument. This is the first impression a listener will have on your playing and will determine your musical voice. This applies to all instruments.

7. **Right notes.** How do I play the correct notes when I improvise? Connecting all aspects of listening, "hear it—sing it—play it," knowledge of chords and scales, using and trusting your ear, and trial and error will all contribute to playing the right notes.

8. **Devices.** Improvisational devices are important. Sequences, patterns, imitation, quotes and snippets of melody are but a few devices you can use in a solo. They work—use these devices and concepts.

9. **Improvisation Tips.** Refer to helpful Improvisation Tips located in the back of this book. There are references in the Improvisation Tips to Roman numerals. These refer to scale tones for the chords. Upper case numerals are major chords, lower case are minor chords.

How to use the mp3 CD (Play the mp3 in your computer)

Learn the tunes by listening, then playing along. Listen to, play and practice the sample solos and then solo over the chord progressions.

1. **Demo Track:** Piano, bass and drumset players can use the Demo track as a demonstration of what/how to play and comp behind the melody, behind a sample jazz solo and how to interact with the other rhythm section players. Listen and learn!

2. **Play-Along Track:** Piano, bass and drumset play along with this track. There is a Play-Along track for piano, bass and drums for each tune with each instrument removed from the mix. YOU comp or play behind the melody, sample jazz solo, and improvise and/or play with the other rhythm section players.

3. **The Sample Solo:** The written-out solos are examples of typical jazz solos based on the chord progression of the tune. The solos incorporate a variety of soloistic devices such as patterns, sequences, quotes, melodic snippets, common licks, non-harmonic passing tones, tension and release, grace notes and so on. Listen to and practice the solos, isolate and imitate ideas in the solos that appeal to you, then apply these ideas to fit over other chord progressions. Observe how the solos are structured and use this structure in your own solos. Some tracks do not have the sample solo played by a horn due to the length of the form. Practice the solos, sing the solos aloud and then close the book and sing from memory. Use your ear!

ALONE TOGETHER

Lyrics by HOWARD DIETZ
Music by ARTHUR SCHWARTZ

8

Solo Composed by
RICH SIGLER

Sample Solo

This page left blank to assist with page turns.

HOW HIGH THE MOON

Music by
MORGAN LEWIS

14

IT'S A RAGGY WALTZ

By DAVE BRUBECK

After Solos, D.S. 𝄋 al Coda

Solo Composed by
RICH SIGLER

SAMPLE SOLO

This page left blank to assist with page turns.

IN YOUR OWN SWEET WAY

By DAVE BRUBECK

Solo Composed by
RICH SIGLER

This page left blank to assist with page turns.

GOOD BAIT

Piano

By TADD DAMERON
and COUNT BASIE

28

Solo Composed by
RICH SIGLER

SAMPLE SOLO

INVITATION

Music by
BRONISLAU KAPER

SAMPLE SOLO

Solo Composed by
RICH SIGLER

(TO BRIDGE)

This page left blank to assist with page turns.

ROBBIN'S NEST

Music by
CHARLES THOMPSON and
ILLINOIS JACQUET

40

AFTER SOLOS, D.S. 𝄋 AL CODA

42

Solo Composed by
RICH SIGLER

UNIT 7

By SAM JONES

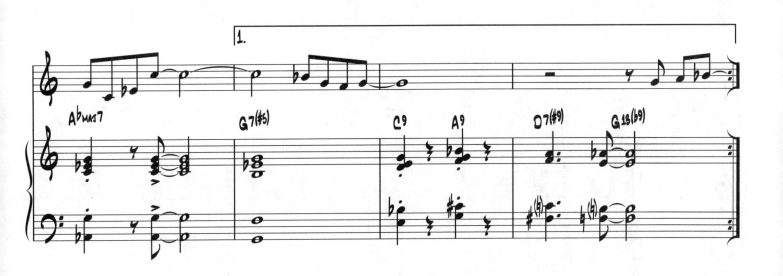

SAMPLE SOLO

Solo Composed by
RICH SIGLER

This page left blank to assist with page turns.

OLD DEVIL MOON

Words by E.Y. HARBURG
Music by BURTON LANE

54

This page left blank to assist with page turns.

ALONE TOGETHER

Lyrics by HOWARD DIETZ
Music by ARTHUR SCHWARTZ

AFTER SOLOS, D.S. % AL CODA

Solo Composed by
RICH SIGLER

HOW HIGH THE MOON

Music by
MORGAN LEWIS

61

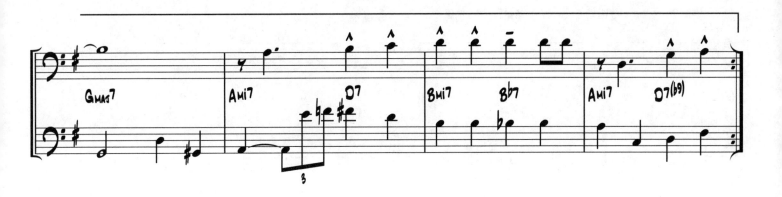

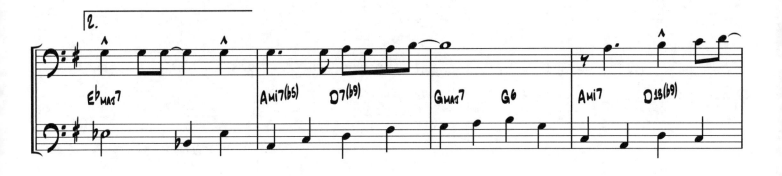

Solo Composed by
RICH SIGLER

IT'S A RAGGY WALTZ

By DAVE BRUBECK

Solo Composed by
RICH SIGLER

This page left blank to assist with page turns.

IN YOUR OWN SWEET WAY

By DAVE BRUBECK

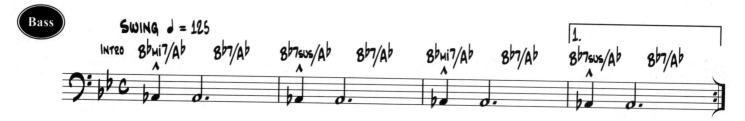

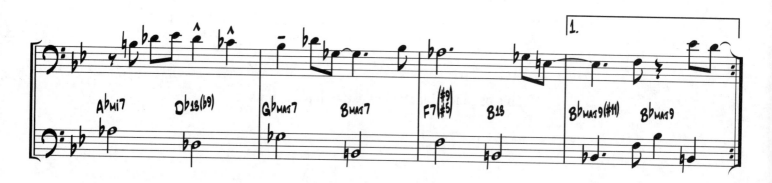

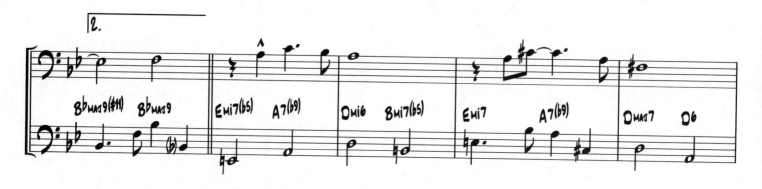

GOOD BAIT

By TADD DAMERON
and COUNT BASIE

Solo Composed by
RICH SIGLER

This page left blank to assist with page turns.

INVITATION

Music by
BRONISLAU KAPER

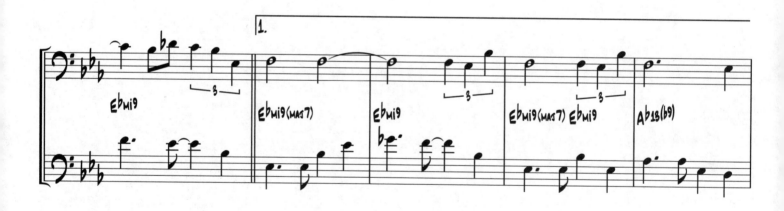

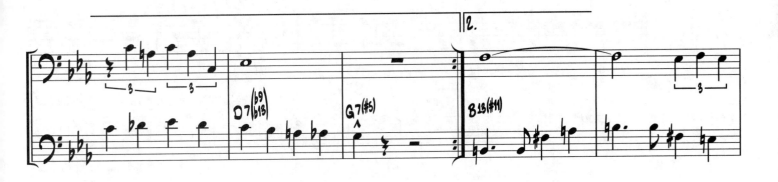

SAMPLE SOLO

Solo Composed by
RICH SIGLER

ROBBIN'S NEST

80

Music by
CHARLES THOMPSON and
ILLINOIS JACQUET

Solo Composed by
RICH SIGLER

SAMPLE SOLO

This page left blank to assist with page turns.

UNIT 7

By SAM JONES

Bass

SWING ♩ = 168

86

Solo Composed by
RICH SIGLER

SAMPLE SOLO

OLD DEVIL MOON

Words by E.Y. HARBURG
Music by BURTON LANE

Swing ♩ = 162

89

Solo Composed by
RICH SIGLER

ALONE TOGETHER

Lyrics by HOWARD DIETZ
Music by ARTHUR SCHWARTZ

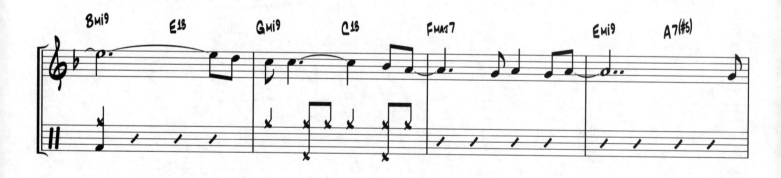

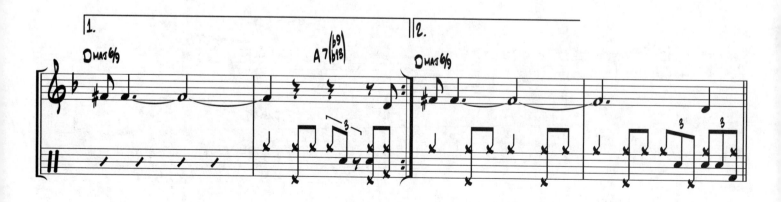

94

Solo Composed by
RICH SIGLER

HOW HIGH THE MOON

Music by
MORGAN LEWIS

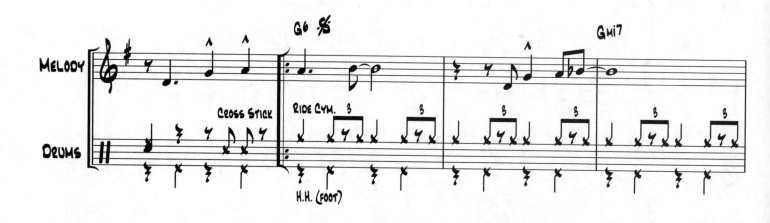

98

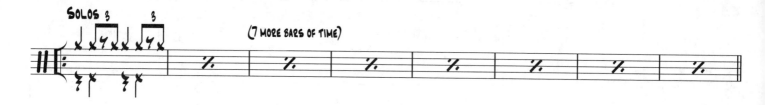

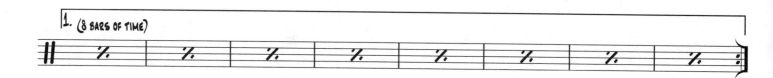

AFTER SOLOS, D.S. 𝄋 AL CODA

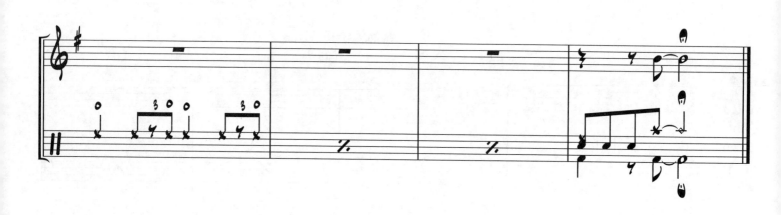

Solo Composed by
RICH SIGLER

SAMPLE SOLO

IT'S A RAGGY WALTZ

By DAVE BRUBECK

SOLOS

(11 MORE BARS OF TIME)

BRIDGE 8 BARS TIME

12 BARS TIME

AFTER SOLOS, D.S. 𝄋 AL CODA

CODA

G   G7   C/G   G

This page left blank to assist with page turns.

IN YOUR OWN SWEET WAY

By DAVE BRUBECK

SOLOS

(4 MORE BARS TIME)

1.

2.   BRIDGE (8 BARS TIME)

(8 BARS TIME)

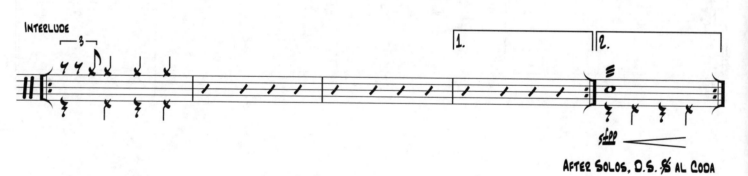

INTERLUDE

1.   2.

sfpp

AFTER SOLOS, D.S. % AL CODA

CODA   F7(#9)(#5)   B13   B♭maj9(#11)

Solo Composed by
RICH SIGLER

GOOD BAIT

By TADD DAMERON
and COUNT BASIE

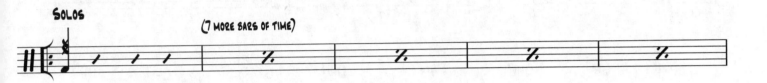

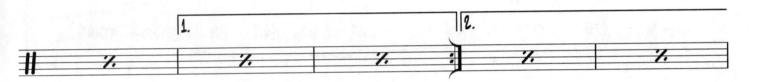

AFTER SOLOS, D.S. %/. AL CODA

Solo Composed by
RICH SIGLER

SAMPLE SOLO

This page left blank to assist with page turns.

INVITATION

Music by
BRONISLAU KAPER

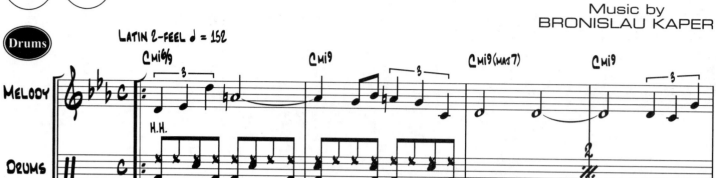

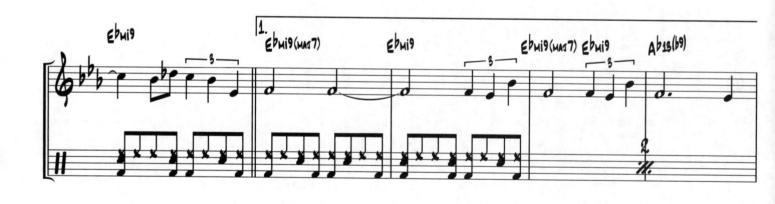

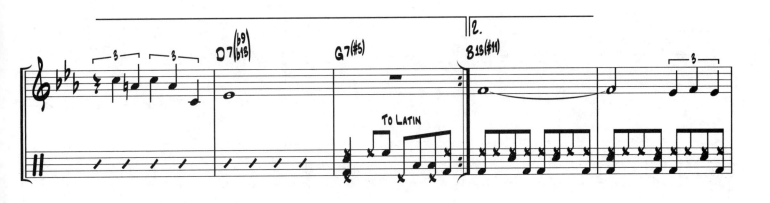

SOLOS

SAMPLE SOLO

(TO BRIDGE)

ROBBIN'S NEST

Music by
CHARLES THOMPSON and
ILLINOIS JACQUET

118

SAMPLE SOLO

Solo Composed by
RICH SIGLER

This page left blank to assist with page turns.

UNIT 7

By SAM JONES

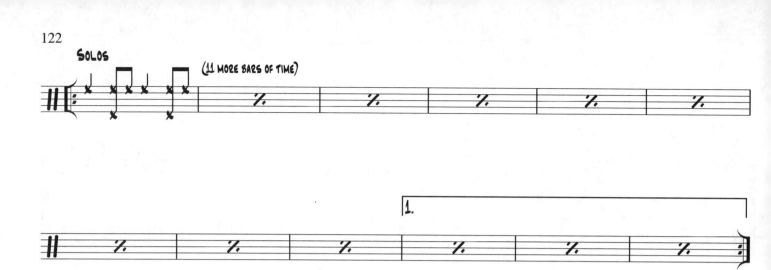

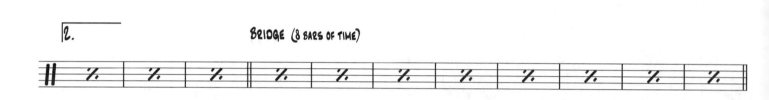

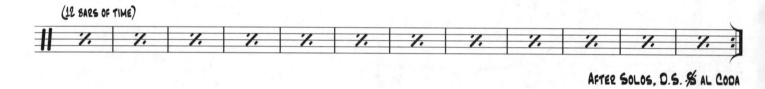

SAMPLE SOLO

Solo Composed by
RICH SIGLER

OLD DEVIL MOON

Words by E.Y. HARBURG
Music by BURTON LANE

SOLOS

(15 MORE BARS OF TIME)

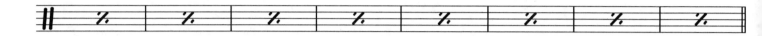

1. (8 BARS OF TIME)

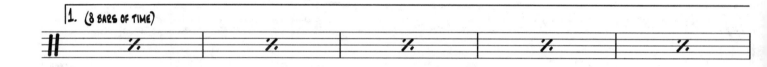

2. (8 BARS OF TIME)

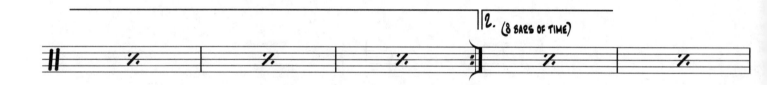

AFTER SOLOS, D.S. 𝄋 AL CODA

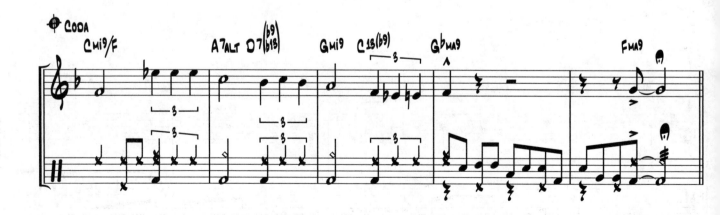

Coda

Cmi9/F   A7ALT D7(b9)(b13)   Gmi9 C13(b9)   GbMA9   FMA9

Solo Composed by
RICH SIGLER

GUITAR CHORD FRAMES

GUITAR CHORDS

These are the most common jazz guitar chord voicings. The root of each chord is circled. Each of these chord fingerings is moveable throughout the neck of the guitar. Whatever note the root is will be the name of the chord. For example, play the first maj7 fingering at the 3rd fret and it will be a Cmaj7, but move it up to the 4th fret and it will be a C#maj7, and so on up the neck.

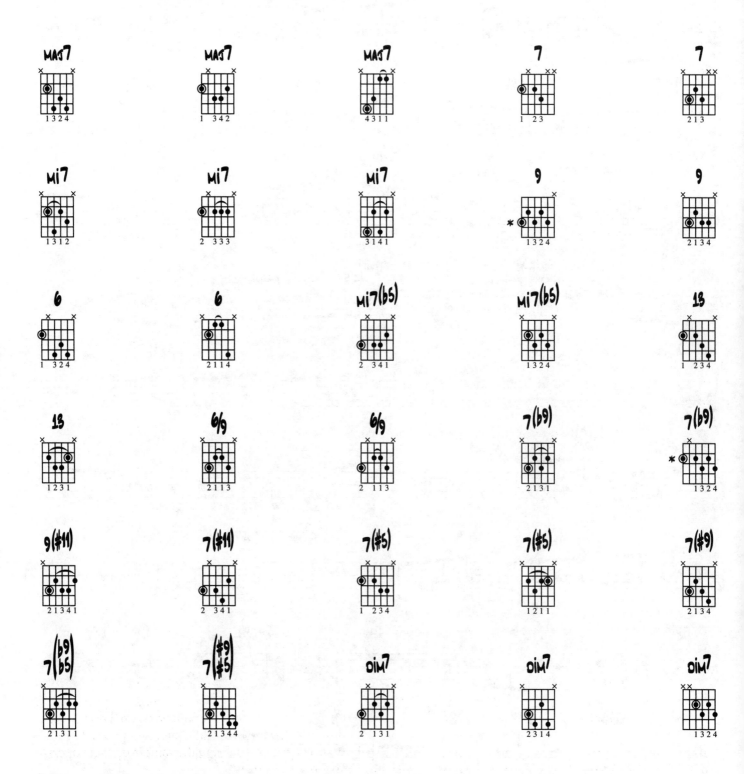

* Do not play the root.

VOL. 1: BRUBECK & MORE
IMPROVISATION TIPS

Chord and note references are in concert key.

Alone Together *(played four times)*

1. This tune has an AABA form, but be aware that the two front A sections are 14 bars. The bridge is 8 bars and the last A section is only 8 bars. The extra measures in the first A sections can be tricky.

2. **Piano**—Vary the comping behind soloists. Keep it supportive and interesting. Always think about leading tones to the next chord in the harmony.

3. **Bass**—A steady walking groove fits this tune. Study the written bass lines behind the melody and the solo section. Notice how the leading tones in the bass lines move the ear into the next chord. Bass lines should provide great time and the tonal foundation plus, direct the music into the chord progression.

4. **Drumset**—Listen to the demo recording to hear how the drummer's ride cymbal and the bass player are locked together. Sometimes easier said than done! This connection is essential to a solid swing feel and groove. Position yourself and the bass player so you can easily hear and see each other. Listen to the subtle unwritten fills and lead-ins to sections of a tune. Be musical.

5. For improvisation, the D minor key portrays a dark sound, but a series of ii-V chords brightens the sound up. Interestingly, the A sections resolve to D major. Try using the Dorian scale for the minor 7th chord: W-H-W-W-W-H-W and Mixolydian scale for the Dominant V7 chord: W-W-H-W-W-H-W.

6. The bridge begins with a ii-V progression in G minor, then ii-V in F major. The minor 7 (♭5) chords are half-diminished chords—a diminished triad with a minor 7th. Try a Locrian scale using these intervals: H-W-W-H-W-W-W— it is very effective for a half-diminished chord.

7. Always feel free to quote the melody in your solo.

8. Begin your improvisation on a different note each time.

How High the Moon *(played four times)*

1. This tune is 32 bars with two A sections, A and A-prime. A-prime is a variation on the first A section.

2. This tune was originally conceived as a ballad but evolved into an up-tempo swing bebop standard.

3. **Piano**—Check out the intro and the coda, both have specific (arranged) piano parts. The swing groove comp that is written is a solid sample of typical comping appropriate for this tune. It is always best for a pianist to be familiar with the tune and the changes to comp effectively. Even though G is the standard key for this tune, many vocalists and instrumentalists will perform tunes in other keys. Be ready by learning tunes in other keys.

4. **Bass**—The intro is arranged along with the piano and drum parts. The written bass part has a relaxed 2-feel behind the melody bouncing occasionally between a

2 and 4-feel. The solo section is a walking 4-feel. When walking a straight 4-feel, intersperse the quarter notes with some triplets or dotted eighth-sixteenths for variety and interest.

5. **Drumset**—The intro is arranged, play the hi-hat. Behind the melody, play a relaxed swing 2-feel with the bass player leading the way. Then swing on the ride in the solo section. Listen to the demo recording for ideas and tips on subtle drumset techniques and how to play with the bass and piano players. Always strive to provide and maintain an interesting groove.

6. For improvisation, the tune begins in G major, but moves to G minor which becomes the ii chord in a ii-V progression to F major followed by the same pattern in E♭.

7. Notice there are minor 7th chords, try the Dorian scale: W-H-W-W-W-H-W. There are also a few minor 7 (♭5) half-diminished chords where you can use the Locrian scale: H-W-W-H-W-W-W.

8. Practice the appropriate scales and chords—be ready to apply your skills to play these chord progressions with ease and confidence.

9. Learn the sample jazz solo and integrate a few ideas and licks from this solo into your improvisation. Listen, study, learn and imitate to broaden your jazz vocabulary.

10. Vary the rhythm in your improvisation to increase the rhythmic interest in your solos. And don't forget the use of space in your solos.

It's a Raggy Waltz *(played four times)*

1. ABA form. The two A sections are 12 bars and the B section is 8 bars.

2. Important note: the form of the written melody includes a D.S. al Fine.

3. As the title suggests, there is a ragtime flavor to the accompaniment to the melody, plus it has a rhythmic feel of a 2 against 3 feel in places. This is classic and creative Brubeck.

4. **Piano**—For the melody, the rag flavor is strongly suggested in the written part. Listen to the demo recording for ideas on interpretation. The solo section is a looser jazz waltz. A key element of the jazz waltz is the lilt or bounce that comes from the "and" of beat 1. If you can lock in this feel, you'll have the jazz waltz groove.

5. **Bass**—The written bass part behind the melody is specific and supports the piano part and the melody. The solo section has a looser feel. Listen to the solo choruses to hear how the bass player walks a swing feel in 3. Listen, learn then imitate. Always support the rhythm section first and foremost.

6. **Drumset**—The written part is specific behind the melody. Listen to the demo, study the music and imitate the feel. It's relaxed groove yet it supports the piano and the bass part. The solo section is a swing feel in 3. The drumset player may consider improvising on a keyboard or mallet instrument using the sample jazz solo or create your own solo ideas.

7. For improvisation, in the sixth measure of the solo section, dig into the C#dim7 chord. This is a fully diminished chord built on minor 3rds. Practice the diminished chords, there are only 3 different diminished chords.

8. Like the sample jazz solo, try beginning your solo with a simple statement, then develop your ideas and build intensity.

9. Begin your improvisation on a different note each time.

In Your Own Sweet Way (played three times)

1. This tune is AABA 32-bar form. However, there is an 8-bar interlude that occurs at the beginning and between each chorus.

2. After the sample jazz solo, the recorded track returns directly back to the melody and coda.

3. **Piano**—It's very important that the form be respected in this tune, especially the interlude. Maintain the half-note feel in the interlude section to keep it "floating" or with a relaxed feel. The melody has a 2-feel and the solo section is straight ahead swing with a typical comp.

4. **Bass**—The interlude has a specific written part for the bass. Behind the melody, there is a 2-feel with half notes to keep the time feel relaxed. Then after the next interlude, dig in with the walking bass line. Listen to the demo recording for style and interpretation suggestions.

5. **Drumset**—Maintain the 2-feel in the interlude and behind the melody, then go the ride cymbal for a solid swing feel in the solo section. Listen closely to the demo recording for subtle drum technique. Listen, learn and apply ideas you like to your playing right away.

6. For improvisation, the interlude has Ab "sus" or suspended chords. Suspended chords do not have an interval of a 3rd, instead, the 4th replaces the 3rd. Throughout this interlude, there is a passing-tone line moving in half-notes from Db to D to Eb and back. The sus chords are often written in different ways, in this case, Bbmi7 with an Ab in the bass, notated as: Bbmi7/Ab.

7. Another feature of this tune is at the end of the A sections, there is a Bbmaj9 (#11) chord that resolves to a Bbmaj9. The melody has a passing tone E to F which creates a brief harmonic dissonance then resolves. A very useful device for tension and release.

8. Like many tune, the chord progression is full of ii-V chord progressions. Practice your ii-V patterns, learn them in all keys, and then apply them right away to your improvisations.

9. The bridge begins with a half-diminished chord, Emi7(b5). Try the Locrian scale: H-W-W-H-W-W-W. For the other minor 7th chords, consider the Dorian scale: W-H-W-W-W-H-W.

10. In the sample jazz solo, measures 17–20 demonstrate a sequence. A sequence is a restatement of the notes or lick at a higher or lower pitch. A useful device—apply it to your solos.

11. The sample solo provides insight into the tune. Listen and study how the sample jazz solo tackles the challenging chord changes. Imitate and integrate these ideas into your solos.

Good Bait (played four times)

1. AABA 32-bar form.

2. The A sections have a typical bebop chord progression similar to the A section of "I Got Rhythm."

3. **Piano**—Standard swing comp style applies all the way in this tune. Note the rhythmic figures in the 1st and 2nd endings with the bass and drumset.

4. **Bass**—Swing 4 all the way. Catch the figures in the 1st and 2nd endings with piano and drumset.

5. **Drumset**—Play a swing ride cymbal groove. Catch the figures in the 1st and 2nd endings with piano and bass. Listen to the demo recording to hear how the drummer compliments the soloist and the other rhythm section players. Keep the energy going but don't rush. For improvisation, consider improvising on a keyboard or mallets using the sample jazz solo or create your own solo ideas.

6. For improvisation, in an interesting twist, the B section mirrors the A section up a fourth in Eb ending with an F7 Dominant chord to bring the harmony back to Bb for the last A section.

7. The A section chord progression has a lot of chordal movement. To gain skill and the confidence to master this progression, begin by playing only the chord roots. Then, when comfortable, work on playing the 3rd of each chord, the 5th and so on. It is a learning process, take it step by step.

8. Write out the arpeggios to each chord and related scales, then apply these skills right away to your improvisation.

9. It's okay to quote the melody in your solo.

10. Begin your improvisation on a different note each time

Invitation (played 2½ times)

1. This tune is basically an ABA form with each section 16 bars in length.

2. **Piano**—This tune is especially fun for the rhythm section because of the transitions from Latin bossa to swing. The written Latin comp shows up-beat syncopation to add energy and forward motion to the bossa feel. Keep in mind the Latin section is played with even eighth notes.

3. **Bass**—The Latin bossa sections have a typical dotted quarter-eighth rhythm pattern. The swing sections walk. Listen and observe how the written bass lines outline the chord foundation and then lead into the next chord. Imitate these bass lines to develop your own style and skills.

4. **Drumset**—Latin, swing, Latin, swing. Maintain the groove throughout and be ready to transition. Listen to the demo recording for tips.

5. For improvisation, the drumset player may consider keyboard or mallets using the sample jazz solo or create your own solo ideas.

6. For improvisation, the 16-bar A sections have 8 bars in C minor, then 8 bars in E♭ minor.

7. The bridge is ii-V-i in B minor, then ii-V-i in A minor, and then again in G minor followed by a transition back to C minor.

8. In the A sections, because of the extended C minor and E♭ minor chords, try introducing a few non-harmonic passing tones—notes not in the chord, but when used as passing tones, will provide an interesting harmonic contrast and color. The sample jazz solo has examples of this device. Check it out, practice it and apply the ideas to your solos. Examples of color tones are: ♭9, ♯9, ♭5, 11ths and ♯11ths.

9. You can try some simple quotes as a device.

10. The bridge will offer you many opportunities to apply ii-V-i patterns. Practice these patterns in major and minor keys so you are confident and can apply these skills to your solos.

11. Try to build a perfectly shaped solo, starting simple, building to a peak and then bringing it back down to finish.

Robbin's Nest *(played four times)*.

1. The form is AABA, with each section 8 bars in length.

2. **Piano**—The intro has an arranged written-out part. Behind the melody, there is accented figure on the "and" of beat 4 in the fourth measure of the melody—catch that accent with the bass and drumset. Listen, learn and imitate from the demo recording to hear how the pianist varies from the written part but always continues to support the melody or soloist.

3. **Bass**—The intro is arranged, play the written part. Behind the melody, there is a 2-feel, then swing in 4 in the solo section. Behind the melody, there is accented figure on the "and" of beat 4 in the fourth measure of the melody—catch that accent with the piano and drumset. Study the written bass lines to get a few ideas to help you create your own solid bass lines.

4. **Drumset**—Play the written intro with the bass and piano. Then a relaxed 2-feel behind the melody. Then swing 4 in the solo section. Behind the melody, there is accented figure on the "and" of beat 4 in the fourth measure of the melody—catch that accent with the bass, piano and horn. Listen to the demo for great ideas the drummer introduces to the groove. Imitate the ideas you hear and apply them to your playing.

5. For improvisation, the A section chord progression has an A♭7 Dominant chord in measures 3–4, you can try using the Mixolydian scale: W-W-H-W-W-H-W.

6. The A sections also feature a descending chord progression in measures 5 and 6. Try some sequences over these chords. Play the same lick over each descending chord but restate the notes at the lower pitch as the chords descend. It's also good ear training.

7. The bridge is basically four Dominant chords, E7, A7, D7 and G7. Each of these chords also has a ♭9 indicated as an extension in the chord. Locate the ♭9 in the chord, listen

for it, practice it and apply it to your solos—it's a great color tone.

8. Check out the sequence in the sample jazz solo, measures 9–12. Integrate this device to your solos.

9. It's okay to quote the melody in your solo.

10. Begin your improvisation on a different note each time

Unit 7 *(played four times)*

1. This tune is AABA. The A sections are 12-bar blues, and the bridge is 8 bars. In a nutshell, it's blues with a bridge.

2. **Piano**—Play the written rhythms behind the melody, that is the typical comp in this tune. The comp behind the solos is looser with a more traditional swing comp.

3. **Bass**—Although the piano has rhythmical pattern behind the melody, the bass is walking. Study the written bass lines for idea and integrate these ideas into your bass playing.

4. **Drumset**—Listen to the piano comping behind the melody and support that with subtle accents on the ride cymbal. Dig in on the bridge. Listen to the demo recording for the many drumming suggestions and ideas you will hear, and then integrate the ones you like into your playing.

5. For improvisation, the drumset player may consider a keyboard instrument using the sample jazz solo or create your own solo ideas.

6. For improvisation, there are many variations of blues chord progressions. In this blues (in C) progression, in measure 9 of the 12-bar blues, the chord is an A♭7 and a substitute for a Dmi7 or a ii chord. Listen for that chord and make the most of this interesting substitution. Consider using the A♭ Mixolydian scale as it is a Dominant 7th chord: W-W-H-W-W-H-W.

7. In the last A section of the solo chords, there is a variation of the blues progression in the 2nd measures with the F13 to F♯dim7. To make the most of this harmony, learn the diminished chords which are built with minor 3rds—there are only three different diminished chords.

8. The bridge includes a few ii-V chords with a turn-around back to C in the last two measures.

9. Check out the quote in the sample jazz solo in measures 25–27 of the tune "Stranger in Paradise," with an alteration to make it fit this chord progression. A clever quote and a very useful and interesting device. Try it!

10. Try beginning your improvisation on a different note each time.

Old Devil Moon *(played four times)*

1. This tune is 48 bars in length. One analysis of the form would be A and A-prime with each A section 24 bars. This tune can also be ABA-prime depending on how it is analyzed.

2. Using the AA-prime analysis, the second A has a variation on the melody and chords in the last section which makes it A-prime.

3. **Piano**—Play the intro as written. The comp behind the first 8-bars of the A section is similar to the intro pattern, then, it changes to a traditional swing comp in measure 9 of the melody.

4. **Bass**—Play the intro with the written-out bass line part. The bass comp behind the first 8-bars of the A section is similar to the intro patterns, and then it changes to a traditional walking bass line in measure 9 of the melody.

5. **Drumset**—Play the intro as written. The drum comp behind the first 8 bars of the A section is similar to the intro pattern, and then it changes to a traditional swing groove in measure 9 of the melody. Listen to the demo recording for tips.

6. For improvisation, the first 8 bars of the A section is a repetitive chord pattern of F to C minor with an F pedal bass note. Weave in and out of these two chords, then move on to the B♭ major chord in the 9th measure.

7. Check out the ii-V progression in the second part of the A section, dig into these chords. Use your ii-V skills!

8. The real twist in the harmony is in measure 19 of the solo section where is chord is Dmaj7. This is an interesting harmonic departure from the original tonal center. Strive to make the most of this D major chord—it's the D major scale. Know all your major scales inside and out and apply those skill to your solos.

9. Always feel free to quote the melody in your solo. Check out measure 28 of the sample jazz solo where there is a brief melody quote. Quoting excerpts of the melody is always a useful improvisational device. Apply it to your solos.

10. Listen, play and study the sample jazz solos, they demonstrate many valuable soloistic techniques.